CONTENTS

T0025123

Words that look like <u>this</u> can be found in the glossary on page 24.

A SLICE OF SCIENCE

Has anyone told you to avoid sweets? Do you get told to eat more vegetables? You might be wondering: why does it matter what I eat?

Hello! I'm a small scientist. I'm here to teach you about food. Food is very important!

You might have heard the words "healthy diet." A diet is the kinds of food you usually eat. To have a healthy diet, you need to make sure you eat many different kinds of food.

A healthy diet is often called a balanced diet because you eat lots of different types of food.

PORTIONS

How do we <u>measure</u> food? A portion, or serving, is the amount of food a person eats in one sitting.

Sometimes portions are measured in ounces. Use a scale like this to weigh your food.

A portion of food might be one apple, or two to three strawberries.

Different foods have different portion sizes. You should have five servings of fruits and vegetables a day. A serving of fruit is roughly the amount you can fit in the palm of your hand.

WHAT IS PROTEIN?

Protein is something that is found in certain kinds of food. Lots of different parts of the human body need protein, and it is important for all sorts of things.

Let's have a look at some foods that give you lots of protein.

Eggs

Seeds and nuts

Pulses such as beans

Meat and fish

9

LET'S EXPERIMENT!

We will need this mood bar. It will tell us about someone's body. It shows four things — how strong a person is, how ill they feel, how healthy their bones are, and how fast they are growing.

STRENGTH

IMMUNE SYSTEM

BONE TOUGHNESS

GROWTH

STRENGTH

IMMUNE SYSTEM

BONE TOUGHNESS

GROWTH

GO, GO GROWTH

Let's give her chicken. <u>Poultry</u> (such as chicken) and other meats give you lots of protein. Protein is used to build body <u>tissue</u>, so you need it to grow bigger.

People who don't want to eat meat are called vegetarians. On page 20 you'll see vegetarian foods that are full of protein!

Look at the mood bar for this next kid. It looks like his bones are weak. What food shall we give him?

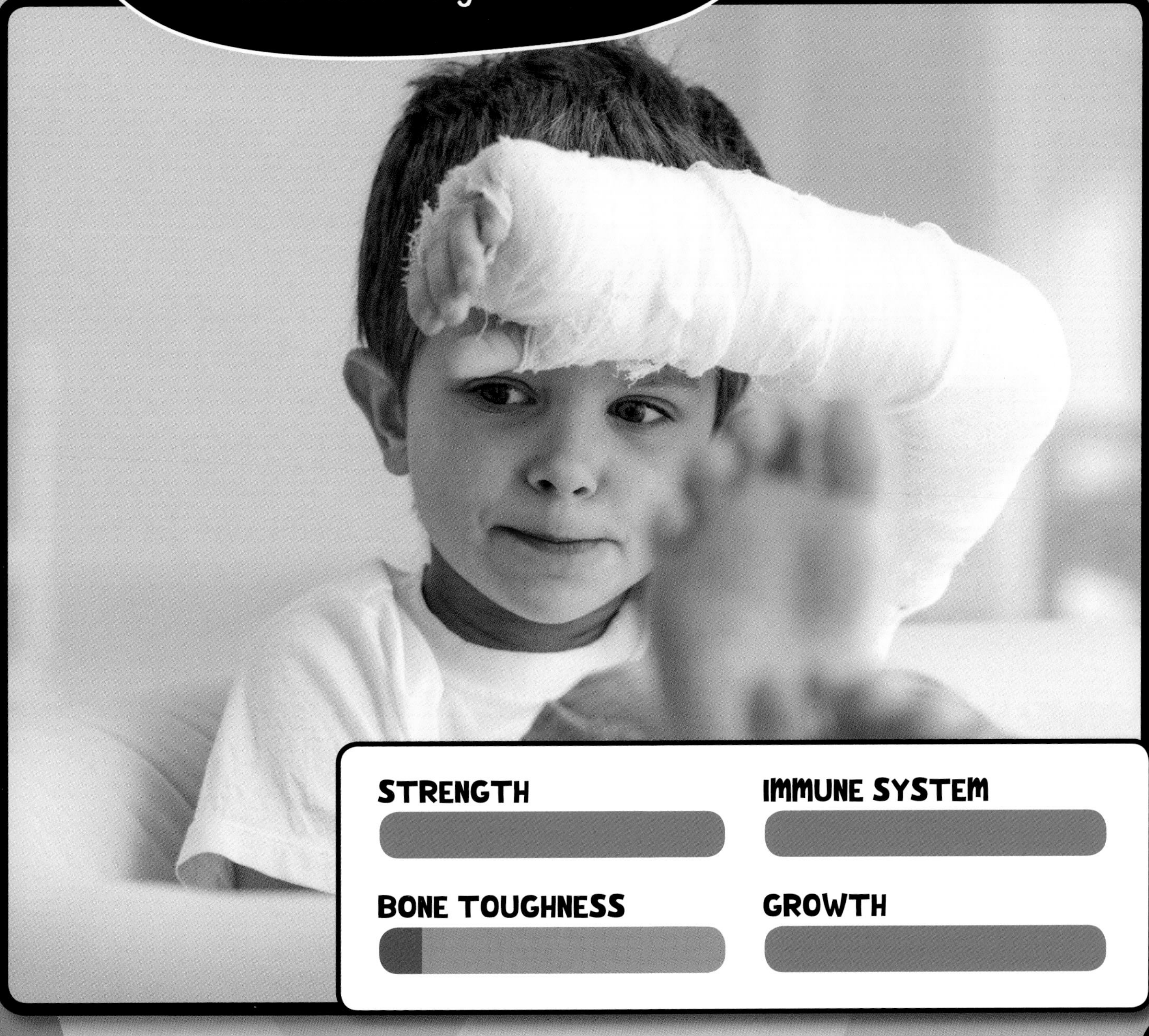

QUICK FIX

He could eat some eggs! As you grow, it is important that your body has all the things it needs to keep your bones strong and healthy. Protein is a very important part of doing that.

People who don't want to eat food that comes from animals are called vegans. Turn to page 20 to see vegan food that is full of protein.

What is the mood bar doing now? It looks like this kid's bones are healthy, but his strength is low! We'd better fix that.
STRENGTH
IMMUNE SYSTEM
BONE TOUGHNESS
GROWTH

FASTER, STRONGER

How about some yogurt and milk? They are full of protein. Protein doesn't make you stronger on its own, but it does help your muscles repair themselves after you _exercise_.

FIGHT THE BLOOD FIGHT

We will give her fish. The body needs protein to fight off <u>infections</u> and make your immune system stronger. One portion of fish has lots of protein.

STRENGTH

IMMUNE SYSTEM

BONE TOUGHNESS

GROWTH

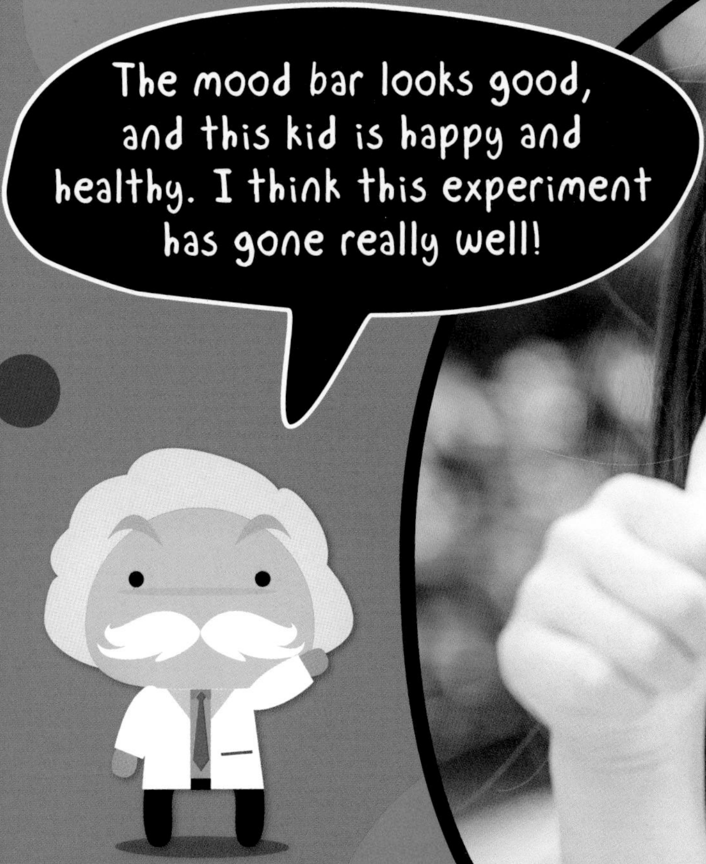

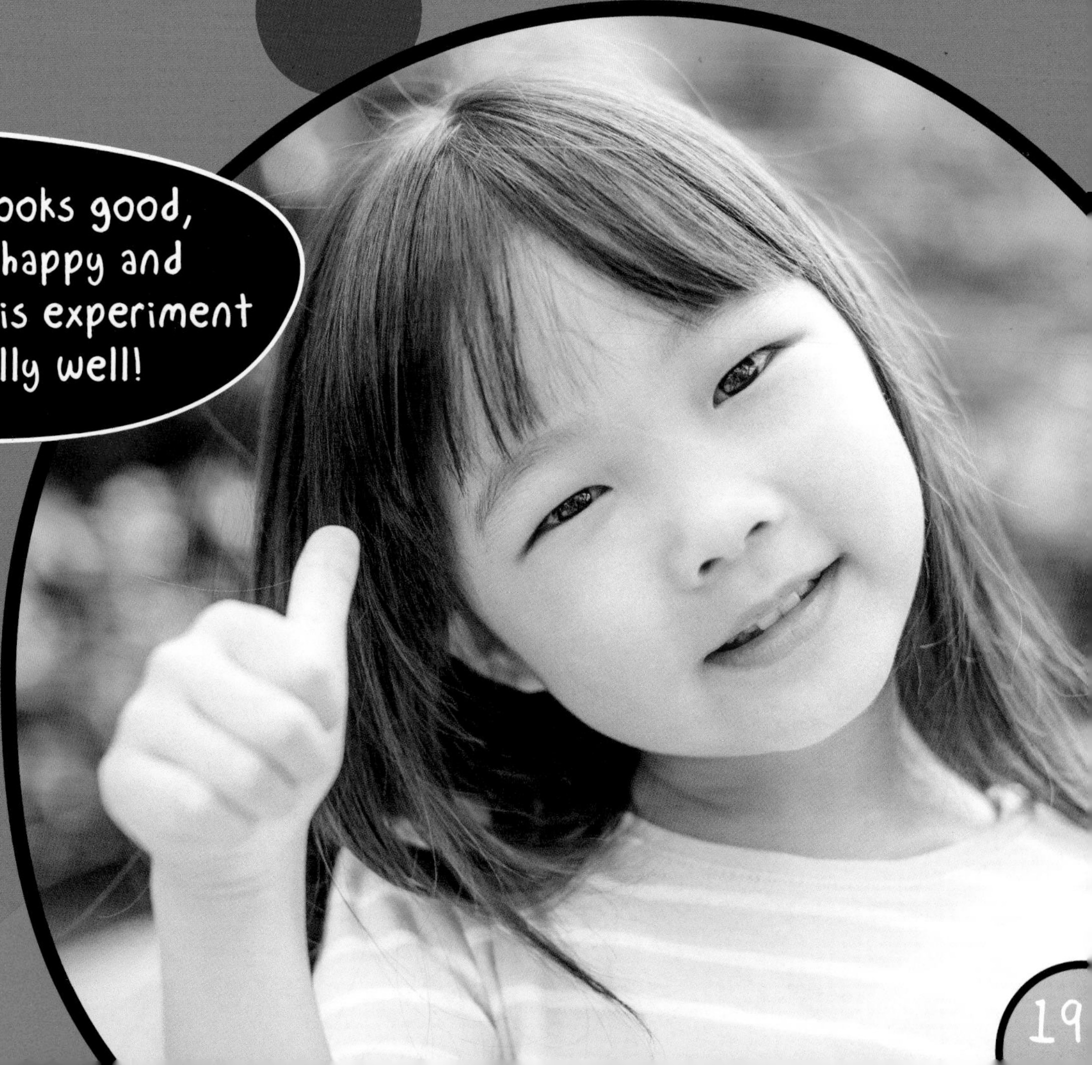

FOOD SWAPS

Lots of people replace meat with tofu.

Some people don't eat animals or anything that comes from animals. Luckily, there are lots of protein-filled foods that come from plants instead!

Soybeans

Lentils

Nuts

Oat milk

Here are more foods with lots of protein.

Chickpeas

Baked beans

Oatmeal

Quinoa

THE MOST IMPORTANT THING

Protein is very good for you, but don't forget that you must eat lots of different types of food.
This is what makes a diet healthy and balanced!

Carbs

Fruits and vegetables

Protein

Fats and sugars

low fat milk

Yogurt

Dairy

GLOSSARY

balanced	made up of the right or equal amounts
exercise	movement done to stay fit and healthy
immune system	the system that our bodies use to defend against illness
infections	illnesses caused by dirt, germs, and bacteria getting into the body
measure	find out the exact amount of something using units or systems, such as ounces for weight or feet for distance
poultry	birds that are raised for meat and eggs, such as chickens
pulses	seeds of certain plants that you can eat, such as peas, beans, and lentils
tissue	groups of cells that are similar to each other and do the same job; muscle tissue and fat tissue are examples of tissues

INDEX